♎ LOVE SIGNS ♎

LIBRA

September 23 – October 23

JULIA & DEREK PARKER

Dedicated to Martin Lethbridge

A DK PUBLISHING BOOK

Project Editor • Annabel Morgan
Art Editor • Anna Benjamin
Managing Editor • Francis Ritter
Managing Art Editor • Derek Coombes
DTP Designer • Cressida Joyce
Production Controller • Martin Croshaw
US Editor • Constance M. Robinson

ACKNOWLEDGMENTS

Photography: Steve Gorton: pp. 10, 13–15, 17–19, 46–49; Ian O'Leary: 16. *Additional photography by:* Colin Keates, David King, Monique Le Luhandre, David Murray, Tim Ridley, Clive Streeter, Harry Taylor, Matthew Ward. *Artworks:* Nic Demin: 34–45; Peter Lawman: *jacket*, 4, 12; Paul Redgrave: 24–33; Satwinder Sehmi: *glyphs*; Jane Thomson: *borders*; Rosemary Woods: 11.

Peter Lawman's paintings are exhibited by the Portal Gallery Ltd, London.

Picture credits: Bridgeman Art Library/Hermitage, St. Petersburg: 51; Robert Harding Picture Library: 201, 20c, 20r; Images Colour Library: 9; The National Gallery, London: 11; The Natural History Museum, London: 49cr; Tony Stone Images: 21t, 21b; The Victoria and Albert Museum, London: 5; Zefa: 21c.

First American Edition, 1996
2 4 6 8 10 9 7 5 3 1

Published in the United States by
DK Publishing, Inc., 95 Madison Avenue, New York, New York 10016
Visit us on the World Wide Web at http://www.dk.com

A catalog record is available from the Library of Congress.

ISBN 0-7894-1095-8

Reproduced by Bright Arts, Hong Kong
Printed and bound by Imago, Hong Kong

CONTENTS

ASTROLOGY & YOU

THERE IS MUCH MORE TO ASTROLOGY THAN YOUR SUN SIGN.
A SIMPLE INVESTIGATION INTO THE POSITION OF THE OTHER
PLANETS AT THE MOMENT OF YOUR BIRTH WILL PROVIDE YOU
WITH FASCINATING INSIGHTS INTO YOUR PERSONALITY.

*Y*our birth sign, or Sun sign, is the sign of the zodiac that the Sun occupied at the moment of your birth. The majority of books on astrology concentrate only on explaining the relevance of the Sun signs. This is a simple form of astrology that can provide you with some interesting but rather general information about you and your personality. In this book, we take you a step further, and reveal how the planets Venus and Mars work in association with your Sun sign to influence your attitudes toward romance and sexuality.

In order to gain a detailed insight into your personality, a "natal" horoscope, or birth chart, is necessary. This details the position of all the planets in our solar system at the moment of your birth, not just the position of the Sun. Just as the Sun occupied one of the 12 zodiac signs when you were born, perhaps making you "a Geminian" or "a Sagittarian," so each of the other planets occupied a certain sign. Each planet governs a different area of your personality, and the planets Venus and Mars are responsible for your attitudes toward love and sex, respectively.

For example, if you are a Sun-sign Sagittarian, according to the attributes of the sign you should be a dynamic, freedom-loving character. However, if Venus occupied Libra when you were born, you may make a passive and clinging partner – qualities that are supposedly completely alien to Sagittarians.

A MAP OF THE CONSTELLATION

The 16th-century astronomer Copernicus first made the revolutionary suggestion that the planets orbit the Sun rather than Earth. In this 17th-century constellation chart, the Sun is shown at the center of the solar system.

The tables on pages 52–61 of this book will enable you to discover the positions of Mars and Venus at the moment of your birth. Once you have read this information, turn to pages 22–45. On these pages we explain how the influences of Venus and Mars interact with the characteristics of your Sun sign. This information will provide you with many illuminating insights into your personality, and explains how the planets have formed your attitudes toward love and sex.

LOOKING FOR A LOVER

ASTROLOGY CAN PROVIDE YOU WITH VALUABLE INFORMATION
ON HOW TO INITIATE AND MAINTAIN RELATIONSHIPS. IT CAN
ALSO TELL YOU HOW COMPATIBLE YOU ARE WITH YOUR LOVER,
AND HOW SUCCESSFUL YOUR RELATIONSHIP IS LIKELY TO BE.

*P*eople frequently use astrology to lead into a relationship, and "What sign are you?" is often used as a conversation opener. Some people simply introduce the subject as an opening gambit, while others place great importance on this question and its answer.

Astrology can affect the way you think and behave when you are in love. It can also provide you with fascinating information about your lovers and your relationships. Astrology cannot tell you who to fall in love with or who to avoid, but it can offer you some very helpful advice.

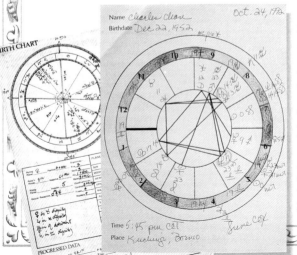

BIRTH CHARTS
Synastry involves the comparison of two people's charts in order to assess their compatibility in all areas of their relationship. The process can highlight any areas of common interest or potential conflict.

THE TABLE OF ELEMENTS

People whose signs are grouped under the same element tend to find it easy to fall into a happy relationship. The groupings are:

FIRE: *Aries, Leo, Sagittarius*
EARTH: *Taurus, Virgo, Capricorn*
AIR: *Gemini, Libra, Aquarius*
WATER: *Cancer, Scorpio, Pisces*

When you meet someone to whom you are attracted, astrology can provide you with a valuable insight into his or her personality. It may even reveal unattractive characteristics that your prospective partner is trying to conceal.

Astrologers are often asked to advise lovers involved in an ongoing relationship, or people who are contemplating a love affair. This important aspect of astrology is called synastry, and involves comparing the birth charts of the two people concerned. Each birth chart records the exact position of the planets at the moment and place of a person's birth.

By interpreting each chart separately, then comparing them, an astrologer can assess the compatibility of any two people, showing where problems may arise in their relationship, and where strong bonds will form.

One of the greatest astrological myths is that people of some signs are not compatible with people of certain other signs. This is completely untrue. Whatever your Sun sign, you can have a happy relationship with a person of any other sign.

YOU & YOUR LOVER

KNOWING ABOUT YOURSELF AND YOUR LOVER IS THE KEY TO
A HAPPY RELATIONSHIP. HERE WE REVEAL THE TRADITIONAL
ASSOCIATIONS OF LIBRA, YOUR COMPATIBILITY WITH ALL THE
SUN SIGNS, AND THE FLOWERS LINKED WITH EACH SIGN.

THE APPLE TREE
IS LINKED WITH
LIBRA AS WELL
AS TAURUS

LIBRAN COLORS
INCLUDE PINK AND
BRIGHT BLUE

THE PLANET
VENUS RULES
OVER THE
SIGN OF LIBRA

DAISIES ARE
TRADITIONALLY
ASSOCIATED
WITH LIBRA

COPPER IS A
LIBRAN METAL

A GRACEFUL,
LONG-LEGGED
STRIDE IS TYPICAL
OF LIBRANS

TORTOISES AND
ALL OTHER
REPTILES ARE
GOVERNED
BY LIBRA

LIBRA AND ARIES

You are tranquil and diplomatic, while Ariens are fiery, active, and decisive. This could prove to be a perfect attraction of opposites, although Arien abrasiveness may rub you the wrong way.

Lavender is a Geminian flower

Thistles are ruled by Aries

LIBRA AND GEMINI

Gregarious, talkative, and easy-going, you will be the most popular couple in the zodiac. However, Gemini can be flighty, and this alliance may not bring you the equilibrium you need.

LIBRA AND TAURUS

Taureans and Librans have much in common. You both love luxury and good living. A warm Taurean will bring you down to earth and provide you with a contented and secure relationship.

The lily, and other white flowers, are ruled by Cancer

The rose is associated with Taurus

LIBRA AND CANCER

You are a lighthearted Libran romantic, whereas Cancerians are much more emotional. You must prove to them that you are serious about your relationship and that they can trust you.

LIBRA AND LEO

A flamboyant, impulsive Leo will breathe new energy and enthusiasm into a languid Libran. Your partnership will be romantic, entertaining, and – last but not least – enduring.

Hydrangeas are governed by Libra

LIBRA AND LIBRA

You will understand each other perfectly, but this is not an ideal match. Neither of you will speak plainly, for fear of hurting the other, and as a couple you may find it difficult to reach decisions.

Sunflowers are ruled by Leo

Honeysuckle is attributed to Scorpio

LIBRA AND VIRGO

You will appreciate the natural refinement of Virgos. They will bring you down to earth, and you will dispel their worries. This should be a happy and enduring relationship.

Small, brightly colored flowers are associated with Virgo

LIBRA AND SCORPIO

You may find the intensity of Scorpio emotions exhausting. You love peace and harmony, while Scorpio thrives on passion. If Scorpio boosts your sex drive, this will be a satisfying union.

LIBRA AND SAGITTARIUS

You make a relaxed and tolerant couple, and will enjoy a cheerful, carefree romance. Sagittarians will help you to become more decisive, and you may persuade them to be a little more tactful.

Orchids are associated with Aquarius

Carnations are ruled by Sagittarius

LIBRA AND CAPRICORN

You may be a little too laid back for an energetic, diligent Capricorn. Once committed, Capricorns are reliable lovers, so this is a safe combination, but one that could lack sparkle.

LIBRA AND AQUARIUS

Aquarius and Libra are both sociable air signs, and you will also share an intellectual rapport. However, as a tactful Libran, you may find Aquarian eccentricity somewhat embarrassing.

Viburnum is governed by Pisces

LIBRA AND PISCES

Libra and Pisces make a sensitive and sympathetic duo. The dreamy emotion of Pisces will soon win your romantic Libran heart, and your tact and diplomacy should allay any Piscean insecurity.

Pansies are Capricorn flowers

THE FOOD OF LOVE

WHEN PLANNING A SEDUCTION, THE SENSUOUS DELIGHTS OF AN
EXQUISITE MEAL SHOULD NEVER BE UNDERESTIMATED. READ ON
TO DISCOVER THE PERFECT MEAL FOR EACH OF THE SUN SIGNS,
GUARANTEED TO AROUSE INTEREST AND STIR DESIRE.

*Librans will
delight in the
delicate flavor
and succulent
texture of asparagus
with hollandaise sauce.*

– THE FOOD OF LOVE –

FOR ARIENS

Spicy mulligatawny soup
·
Peppered steak
·
Baked Alaska

FOR TAUREANS

Cream of cauliflower soup
·
Tournedos Rossini
·
Rich chocolate and brandy mousse

FOR GEMINIANS

Seafood and avocado salad
·
Piquant stir-fried pork with ginger
·
Zabaglione

FOR CANCERIANS

Artichoke vinaigrette
·
Sole Bonne Femme
·
Almond soufflé

FOR LEOS

Roasted tomato and garlic soup
·
Boeuf Stroganoff
·
Pears cooked in wine

FOR VIRGOS

Eggplant salad
·
Paella
·
French apple tart

FOR LIBRANS

Asparagus with hollandaise sauce
·
Pork with roasted apples
·
Strawberry Pavlova

FOR SCORPIOS

Vichyssoise
·
Lobster Newburg
·
Blueberry cream

– THE FOOD OF LOVE –

FOR SAGITTARIANS
Chilled cucumber soup
·
Nutty onion flan
·
Rhubarb crumble with fresh cream

FOR CAPRICORNS
Eggs Florentine
·
Pork tenderloin stuffed with sage
·
Pineapple Pavlova

FOR AQUARIANS
Watercress soup
·
Chicken cooked with chili and lime
·
Lemon soufflé

FOR PISCEANS
French onion soup
·
Trout au vin rosé
·
Melon sorbet

PLACES TO LOVE

ONCE YOU HAVE WON YOUR LOVER'S HEART, A ROMANTIC
VACATION TOGETHER WILL SEAL YOUR LOVE. HERE, YOU
CAN DISCOVER THE PERFECT DESTINATION FOR EACH SUN
SIGN, FROM HISTORIC CITIES TO IDYLLIC BEACHES.

THE
EIFFEL
TOWER,
PARIS

ARIES

*Florence is an Arien
city, and its perfectly
preserved Renaissance
palaces and churches
will set the scene for
wonderful romance.*

TAURUS

*The unspoiled scenery
and unhurried pace
of life in rural Ireland
is sure to appeal to
patient and placid
Taureans.*

GEMINI

*Vivacious and restless
Geminians will feel at
home in the fast-paced
and sophisticated
atmosphere of
New York.*

CANCER

*The watery beauty
and uniquely romantic
atmosphere of Venice
is guaranteed to arouse
passion and stir the
Cancerian imagination.*

ST. BASIL'S
CATHEDRAL,
MOSCOW

AYERS ROCK/ULURU,
AUSTRALIA

LEO

Leos will fall in love all over again when surrounded by the picturesque charm and unspoiled medieval atmosphere of Prague.

VIRGO

Perhaps the most elegant and romantic of all cities, Paris is certainly the ideal setting for a stylish and fastidious Virgo.

LIBRA

The dramatic and exotic beauty of Upper Egypt and the Nile will provide the perfect backdrop for wooing a romantic Libran.

SCORPIO

Intense and passionate Scorpios will be strongly attracted by the whiff of danger present in the exotic atmosphere of New Orleans.

SAGITTARIUS

The wide-ranging spaces of the Australian outback will appeal to the Sagittarian love of freedom and the great outdoors.

CAPRICORN

Capricorns will be fascinated and inspired by the great historical monuments of Moscow, the most powerful of all Russian cities.

AQUARIUS

Intrepid Aquarians will be enthralled and amazed by the unusual sights and spectacular landscapes of the Indian subcontinent.

PISCES

Water-loving Pisceans will be at their most relaxed and romantic by the sea, perhaps on a small and unspoiled Mediterranean island.

THE PYRAMIDS, EGYPT

GONDOLAS, VENICE

THE TAJ MAHAL, INDIA

VENUS & MARS

LUCID, SHINING VENUS AND FIERY, RED MARS HAVE ALWAYS BEEN
ASSOCIATED WITH HUMAN LOVE AND PASSION. THE TWO
PLANETS HAVE A POWERFUL INFLUENCE ON OUR ATTITUDES
TOWARD LOVE, SEX, AND RELATIONSHIPS.

The study of astrology first began long before humankind began to record its own history. The earliest astrological artifacts discovered, scratches on bones recording the phases of the Moon, date from well before the invention of any alphabet or writing system.

The planets Venus and Mars have always been regarded as having enormous significance in astrology. This is evident from the tentative attempts of early astrologers to record the effects of the two planets on humankind. Hundreds of years later, the positions of the planets were carefully noted in personal horoscopes. The earliest known record is dated 410 BC: "Venus [was] in the Bull, and Mars in the Twins."

The bright, shining planet Venus represents the gentle effect of the soul on our physical lives. It is responsible for a refined and romantic sensuality – "pure" love, untainted by sex. Venus reigns over our attitudes toward romance and the spiritual dimension of love.

The planet Mars affects the physical aspects of our lives – our strength, both physical and mental; our endurance; and our ability to fight for survival. Mars is also strongly linked to the sex drive of both men and women. Mars governs our physical energy, sexuality, and levels of desire.

Venus is known as an "inferior" planet, because its orbit falls between Earth and the Sun. Venus orbits the Sun

LOVE CONQUERS ALL

In Botticelli's Venus and Mars, *the warlike, fiery
energy of Mars, the god of war, has been overcome by
the gentle charms of Venus, the goddess of love.*

closely, and its position in the
zodiac is always in a sign near
that of the Sun. As a result, the
planet can only have occupied
one of five given signs at the
time of your birth – your Sun
sign, or the two signs before or
after it. For example, if you were
born with the Sun in Virgo,
Venus can only have occupied
Cancer, Leo, Virgo, Libra, or
Scorpio at that moment.

Mars, on the other hand, is
a "superior" planet. Its orbit lies
on the other side of Earth from

the Sun, and therefore the
planet may have occupied any
of the 12 signs at the moment
of your birth.

On the following pages
(24–45) we provide you with
fascinating insights into how
Mars and Venus govern your
attitudes toward love, sex, and
relationships. To ascertain which
sign of the zodiac the planets
occupied at the moment of
your birth, you must first consult
the tables on pages 52–61. Then
turn to page 24 and read on.

YOUR LOVE LIFE

THE PLANET VENUS REPRESENTS LOVE, HARMONY, AND UNITY.
WORK OUT WHICH SIGN OF THE ZODIAC VENUS OCCUPIED AT
THE MOMENT OF YOUR BIRTH (SEE PAGES 52–57), AND READ ON.

VENUS IN LEO

*V*enus will bring several fiery traits from Leo to spice up your gentle Libran personality. These attributes are likely to be positive ones. You will be very generous and warm-hearted, with a genuine interest and concern for the well-being and happiness of others.

Librans tend to be strongly motivated by their need to form a stable alliance. You will long for a happy and secure permanent relationship, and are prone to feelings of loneliness and inadequacy when single. Your fear of being alone may make you overly anxious if an affair is not going well, or has just ended. There is a danger that you may leap into a new affair as soon as you meet anyone even vaguely suitable. This urge to rush into a relationship before you have gotten to know the other person well may lead to disaster. When you know him or her better, you may find that you are totally unsuited to each other.

In the early stages of an affair, you may shower your potential partner with lavish gifts and attention. Subconsciously, you might think that in this way you can buy long-lasting affection. Do not allow Libran lack of confidence to lead you to try and purchase love. At heart you are extremely responsive and loving. If you show your true character, people will warm to you immediately without needing any material incentives.

The forceful influence of Leo may encourage you to adopt a domineering attitude toward your lover. Do not become too autocratic or try to make decisions for your partner. Even if your advice is very helpful and constructive, it may not be gratefully received. Your partner will be far more appreciative if you display consideration and understanding, and provide a sympathetic ear.

When you find the right partner, all your best qualities will reveal themselves – the supportiveness and kindness of Libra, combined with the enthusiasm and generosity of Leo. Many Librans can be a little lethargic in the bedroom, but Venus from Leo will make you more passionate. You will enjoy sex, and certainly need satisfaction in this area; therefore, you must release any lingering Libran laziness.

VENUS IN VIRGO

*F*rom Virgo, the influence of Venus will make you practical, reliable, and extremely sympathetic. These qualities will combine with your abundance of Libran warmth and affection to make you a very considerate and supportive partner.

Libra will instill in you a deep underlying need for a loving and secure partnership; due to the influence of Virgo you may be shy and introverted when it comes to expressing that need. The Virgoan influence may lessen your self-confidence, but you must try to recognize your own attractiveness. Avoid telling yourself that you are a boring or undesirable person. When you meet someone you are attracted to, you may want him or her to make a move in your direction. However, when someone's interest in you is obvious, your natural shyness may prevent you from responding in kind.

Resolve to make your interest in him or her apparent and react with enthusiasm instead of blushing nervously and giving a brusque rebuff. You must not allow your natural Virgoan shyness to conceal your innate Libran warmth, affection, and interest in others.

You must also avoid going to the opposite extreme, in which you adopt an effusive and gushing manner in an attempt to disguise your shyness. Your bashfulness and self-effacement is something that many people find very endearing and attractive. You should not try to conceal these qualities by behaving in a loud and bombastic fashion that is completely out of character.

Librans are often so eager to form a secure permanent relationship that they throw caution to the wind and fling themselves recklessly into

a liaison without pausing to consider how compatible they are with their potential partner. Fortunately, the discerning and discriminating influence of Virgo should bring you a welcome streak of caution. You will be very sensible and pragmatic and are therefore less likely than other Librans to throw yourself at someone totally unsuitable. This injection of prudence and practicality will be an entirely beneficial addition to your personality, because it will save you from much heartache and disappointment.

When Venus occupies Virgo, the planet may encourage you to criticize, largely due to the fact that Virgo demands perfection from everyone and everything. However, Libra is an extremely diplomatic sign, and any criticisms you make are likely to be tactfully and constructively worded.

VENUS IN LIBRA

*A*ll your natural Libran characteristics, both positive and negative, will be strengthened and intensified when Venus and the Sun work together from Libra.

If both the Sun and Venus occupied Libra at the moment of your birth, you will make a wonderfully supportive partner. You are highly sympathetic and intuitive, and when your lover turns to you for advice, you will happily give all of your time and attention to him or her.

Your whole attitude toward love will be extremely romantic and idealistic; you are seduced by the very idea of being in love. Librans will blossom once they have become involved in a stable and loving relationship, but there is a slight danger that you may be so eager to find a partner that you will throw yourself recklessly at the first person who catches your eye. Of course,

your relationship may work out perfectly, but there is also a possibility that it will not. Try to be more cautious when you are initially attracted to someone. You must take time to consider every aspect of your potential partner's character, and carefully consider how compatible the two of you are likely to be. It would be a good idea for you to experience a couple of relationships before you finally settle down, although this idea may not appeal to you.

Balance and equilibrium are key words for Librans, and you will only be happy if a tranquil atmosphere prevails in your relationships. Sometimes you can be ingratiating in your attempts to keep your friends and lover happy, because emotional upheavals are hard for you to cope with. When a dispute occurs, you tend to distance yourself, try not to become

involved, and hope that the storm will soon blow over. This approach rarely works in a domestic situation, because honest discussion is one of the most important ingredients in a truly secure relationship. Do not agree automatically with everything your lover says in an attempt to avoid argument; your lover may begin to regard your character as weak, superficial, and lacking in integrity.

Again, it is possible that two or three "trial" relationships could help you to develop your own way of dealing with any crises that occur.

Your social skills are likely to be well developed, and you are a charming and urbane addition to any social occasion. Due to the Libran desire to please, you will be extremely popular; you are good at flattery and excel at smoothing ruffled feathers.

VENUS IN SCORPIO

*T*he strong, passionate qualities that Venus brings from Scorpio will overcome the usual Libran tendency toward lethargy and indecision, and will greatly increase your chances of achieving a rewarding and long-lasting relationship.

If Venus occupied Scorpio at the moment of your birth, your intrinsic Libran longing for a secure and happy permanent relationship will be emphasized. This planetary placing will help prevent you from adopting an overly accommodating or ingratiating attitude toward your partner. Therefore, your chances of forming a successful long-term relationship will be greatly increased.

Due to the powerful influence of Scorpio, Venus will inject you with a strong sense of motivation and purpose, and when you meet someone you are attracted to, you will not hesitate. Instead, you will forge straight ahead and make your feelings quite clear. Finding a partner should not present you with any difficulties. You will possess an air of passion and intensity that, when combined with your natural Libran charm, will make you very seductive. From Scorpio Venus will imbue you with a bewitching air of romantic mystery that can be quite irresistible, and you are likely to have an abundance of adoring admirers competing for your favor.

In common with all Librans, a happy permanent relationship is your ideal in life, and you will devote much time and effort to making your partnership work. However, do not allow your determination for it to succeed to spiral out of control. Due to the influence of Scorpio, Venus may introduce a rather claustrophobic atmosphere into

the relationship; you may be overly solicitous, or even jealous and possessive. Keep a sharp eye for these unattractive attributes, or they may begin to infiltrate and poison your relationship. The gentle Libran side of your personality will dislike such qualities and will work hard to suppress them, but the influence of Scorpio is a potent one, and jealousy is an overwhelming emotion.

Venus puts a strong emphasis on sexuality from this sign, and you must find an outlet for your sexual energy. If you can balance the idealistic and peaceful qualities of Libra with the passion and dynamism of Scorpio, you will make a sensitive yet forceful partner. You are capable of creating a relationship that is stable, secure, stimulating, and exciting all at the same time.

VENUS IN SAGITTARIUS

*T*his lively placing of Venus will add a youthful and energetic charm to your personality. You can be flirtatious and lighthearted, but you also possess a passionate and fiery side to your character that will prove irresistibly attractive to everyone who comes into contact with it.

Your partner will find you an enthusiastic and optimistic companion, and you have a talent for encouragement and motivation. You will be more forthright and less gushing and sentimental than many Librans. Due to the Sagittarian influence, you may appear tough and self-sufficient, but romance and a secure and fulfilling long-term relationship are still extremely important to you.

You enjoy excitement and novelty, and may find chasing a potential partner every bit as exciting as the conquest.

Venus in Sagittarius could bring an impulsive and restless side to your personality; to you, the grass may always appear greener on the other side of the fence. As a result, you may find yourself looking around for an exciting new partner before you have terminated the relationship in which you are currently involved. This tendency may also increase your natural Libran indecision. Try not to leap from relationship to relationship in a constant search for the perfect partnership. Not only will you cause much pain to your lovers, but you will also feel unsettled and unbalanced.

Although a permanent relationship is the ideal state for a Libran, Venus will bring you from Sagittarius a love of freedom. The concept of being tied exclusively to one person may give you a few moments of panic. Duality is an integral part

of the Sagittarian nature, and when Venus occupies that sign, this quality will usually manifest itself in some way. This may be as harmless as an occasional need to spend time with friends without your lover. Fortunately, your need for independence should not present a problem. It is more likely to be beneficial by encouraging you not to be too emotionally dependent on one person.

For you, the perfect relationship will be based on intellectual as well as sexual compatibility. You will want your partnership to be a meeting of minds as well as a great physical passion, a personal association that is friendly and companionable as well as romantic. If you try to bear this in mind when searching for a partner, you will achieve a rewarding, long-lasting, and fulfilling relationship.

YOUR SEX LIFE

THE PLANET MARS REPRESENTS PHYSICAL AND SEXUAL ENERGY.
WORK OUT WHICH SIGN OF THE ZODIAC MARS OCCUPIED AT THE
MOMENT OF YOUR BIRTH (SEE PAGES 58–61), AND READ ON.

MARS IN ARIES

*T*he vigorous energy and assertiveness of Mars in Aries will invigorate your rather sluggish sexuality and enable you to express your warm sensuality in a more lively fashion.

Many Librans tend to regard sex as delightful in theory but too much effort in practice. Fortunately, the influence of

Mars will increase your libido and you will be a passionate and energetic lover. However, the diplomatic skills of Libra will ensure that your performance never lacks finesse.

Your passive and easygoing manner will toughen with this placing. Try not to go too far and become dominating.

MARS IN TAURUS

From Taurus, Mars will give a boost to your sex drive and will add a pleasant warmth, sensuality, and affection to your lovemaking.

Librans are not renowned for having abundant energy supplies, but due to the influence of Taurus you will have plenty of stamina. When it comes to sexual activity you will adopt a sensual and leisurely approach. As a result you will be a skilled and expert lover, and will fulfill and stimulate your partner.

When Mars shines from Taurus, you may be prone to abrupt outbursts of anger. This is uncharacteristic of Librans, who usually go out of their way to avoid disputes and disagreements. However, when annoyed, Taurus tends to smolder with rage until an explosion is unexpectedly triggered off. When you lose your temper, your lover may be surprised by the violence of your rage. Try to control yourself and do not fly off the handle; your fury can be intimidating.

MARS IN GEMINI

*W*hen Mars shines from Gemini, you will find sex enormous fun and greatly enjoy playing the tantalizing game of courtship and seduction. You will enjoy an active sex life, and your lovemaking will be skillful and highly imaginative.

A serious and stable emotional relationship is the central focus of the Libran personality. Gemini, however, is a sign associated with duality, and you may find that you are not content with just one partner. You enjoy flirting,

but hopefully the Libran influence will prevent you from straying into infidelity.

Due to the influence of Gemini, Mars may make you restless or encourage you to make sudden changes of direction. This will promote the changeable side of your Libran personality, which is never far beneath the surface. Unexpected changes of mind and opinion can be confusing for your partner and friends; therefore, try not to become too unpredictable.

– YOUR SEX LIFE –

MARS IN CANCER

*C*ancer is a demonstrative and emotional sign, and this placing will make you even more protective and caring than your fellow Librans. You may find that your emotional energy is stronger than your physical energy and your interest in sex.

However, once your interest is aroused and your sexual appetite is awakened, you will be a passionate and sensual lover. You will be instinctively aware of your partner's needs and will work hard to satisfy them.

Due to the touchy and sensitive influence of Cancer, you may find it hard to forgive and forget in the aftermath of a quarrel. You may appear sulky, and as if you are bearing a grudge. Underneath, however, you will long to let bygones be bygones and will loathe the resentment you find yourself harboring. Luckily, Librans tend to be easy-going and relaxed; therefore, you should not find it too difficult to deal with any bad moods brought on by Mars in Cancer.

MARS IN LEO

The bold and forceful influence of Mars in Leo will heighten your enthusiasm and energy, making you a more dynamic and exuberant companion than many Librans.

Librans can feel unfulfilled and lonely when they are not involved in a secure long-term relationship. Once you have found the right partner and made a serious commitment, you will be intensely faithful, loyal, and supportive, and should enjoy a long and happy liaison.

You will work hard to keep your lover happy and fulfilled within your relationship. Although your sex life may not be very wild or experimental, you will be a passionate and generous lover. Due to the luxury-loving influence of Leo, you will be determined to woo your lover in the most elegant of surroundings.

All Librans revel in love and romance, but do not spoil your lover too much, because your abundance of charms might begin to be taken for granted.

MARS IN VIRGO

From Mars, the Virgoan influence can result in shyness and inhibition. In addition, your rather lukewarm Libran energy supply tends to fall off when it comes to sexual activity, and your sex life may be rather subdued.

However, Mars in this sign will also bring you a warm and earthy sensuality. Once aroused you will be a surprisingly ardent lover, provided you do not allow Libran lethargy or Virgoan shyness to cool your sex drive.

Due to your Libran Sun sign, one of your greatest aims is to form a successful permanent relationship. In contrast, Virgo is a very discriminating sign, and Mars may communicate some of this fastidiousness to you. As a result, you may find that you have some difficulty in finding someone who measures up to your high standards. Try not to let inherent Virgoan perfectionism prevent you from forming a satisfying and fulfilling long-term partnership.

MARS IN LIBRA

*O*nce you are aroused your partner will not have any complaints; your sexuality will be heightened by this placing of the planet, and you may find it easier to relax and enjoy yourself than some of your fellow Librans.

Libra can be rather lethargic, and from this placing Mars will not be able to combat your tendency towards inactivity. Vigorous exercise is unlikely to appeal to you, and you may possess a rather lukewarm attitude to sex. You may even find excuses to avoid making love. Remember, there is a limit to the number of headaches you can feign in a week.

Librans are extremely romantic and can feel incomplete without a partner. You may be so eager to form a permanent relationship that you fling yourself into affairs with abandon. Try not to be too idealistic or impulsive, because a failed affair will cause you much heartache and disillusionment.

MARS IN SCORPIO

*T*his is a vigorous and forceful combination, due to the strong alliance between Mars and Scorpio. Assertive, fiery Mars will bring the energy of Scorpio to the laid-back sexual personality of Libra, and as a result you will be a passionate and exciting lover.

Librans can be sluggish and lethargic, but when Mars shines from Scorpio, your libido will receive a welcome boost. You must find a satisfying outlet for your powerful sexuality.

Everyone needs sexual fulfillment, but for a Libran with Mars in Scorpio, any failure to achieve the pinnacle of pleasure could be extremely frustrating.

Due to the influence of Scorpio, you may find that you can be unreasonably jealous. If you experience any pangs of this destructive emotion, squelch them firmly. This minor problem aside, there is wonderful potential in this planetary placing, and you will be among the most dynamic, energetic, and skillful of lovers.

MARS IN SAGITTARIUS

This lively combination gives an enormous boost to to the physical energy, which will be very beneficial for Sun-sign Librans. Your sexuality will be invigorated, and as a result your lovemaking should be energetic and adventurous.

From Sagittarius, Mars may bring an element of duality to your personality, and you may have a tendency to enjoy more than one relationship at a time. In addition, you are restless and easily bored. You tend to lose interest in a project before it is finished, moving on to a new one, only to become bored again and repeat the pattern.

This may also be true of your emotional relationships. Try not to become involved with a new lover before you have finished with the old one, because you may unintentionally cause a great deal of confusion and heartbreak. A partner who can stimulate your mind and match your enjoyment of sex will be the perfect match for you.

MARS IN CAPRICORN

*W*hen Mars shines from Capricorn, one of your primary motivations in life will be the will to win, to come first in any competition. This is an unusual trait for Librans, because they are not usually competitive or ambitious types.

The forceful and determined influence of Capricorn will soon overpower any Libran indecision or lethargy. When attracted to someone, you will not sit back and let him or her decide whether to approach you. You will make the first move, and your determination is likely to win the heart of any potential lover.

There is a danger that you may devote all your redoubtable energies to your career. If you want to achieve a satisfying emotional relationship, you must sometimes sacrifice your worldly ambition to love. Capricorns want to excel at anything they undertake, so you will aim to be an accomplished lover, and your partner will revel in your expert lovemaking techniques.

MARS IN AQUARIUS

The quirky influence of Aquarius will make you an original and inventive lover, and your unpredictability is guaranteed to keep your partner stimulated. You will greatly enjoy sex and will be eager to experiment, although the Libran influence may slightly dampen your erotic energy.

Librans are at their happiest and most fulfilled when they become involved in a successful and stable permanent relationship. However, Aquarius is an independent and freedom-loving sign, and when you enter into an affair you may experience a most uncharacteristic reluctance to become seriously involved. If your partner hints that a long-term commitment is his or her goal, you may not be able to prevent yourself from recoiling.

Remember that Librans are at their happiest in a permanent relationship. Do not allow the Aquarian influence to hold you back from entering into a long-term partnership.

MARS IN PISCES

*D*ue to the influence of Mars in Pisces, you will be a sensual and passionate lover, and your emotional temperature will be raised to a fever pitch. Sex plays an important role in your emotional relationships, and to you it signifies the ultimate union with a partner.

You must ensure that your abundance of emotional and sexual energy is rewardingly and imaginatively directed. Any obstacle that inhibits the flow of such a strong force may cause frustration and lack of fulfillment. A lively and regular sex life is likely to keep you stimulated and contented.

In the midst of all the pleasures of a love affair, look coolly at your relationship and evaluate its progress. The Piscean influence might prompt you to form a relationship on the grounds of sexual compatibility alone, but such unions are unlikely to be well balanced. You need to find a partner who will be a friend as well as a lover.

TOKENS OF LOVE

ASTROLOGY CAN GIVE YOU A FASCINATING INSIGHT INTO YOUR LOVER'S PERSONALITY AND ATTITUDE TOWARD LOVE. IT CAN ALSO PROVIDE YOU WITH SOME INVALUABLE HINTS WHEN YOU WANT TO CHOOSE THE PERFECT GIFT FOR YOUR LOVER.

ARIES

Ariens tend to be very active, and sports equipment is sure to please. Instead of chocolates, give Ariens ginger preserve because they relish warm, spicy foods.

TABLE TENNIS BALLS

GEMINI

A handsome box of Jordan almonds or exotic nuts will be greatly appreciated by your Geminian lover.

CRYSTALLIZED CHESTNUTS

TAURUS

Taureans value quality above quantity. Hand-painted porcelain will appeal, as will hand-made chocolates, or perhaps a rich chocolate cake.

CHOCOLATE CAKE

ANTIQUE CHINESE
SNUFF BOTTLE

NATURAL
PEARLS

CANCER

Cancerians adore
unusual curios. Pearl
is the Cancerian
gemstone, and any
jewelry or accessories
decorated with pearls
will be cherished forever.

OIL
PAINTING

GOLD
KEY RING

LEO

Gold-colored
objects will
delight your
Leo lover, because gold is
the Leo metal. An original
painting is sure to appeal.
Sunflowers are also ruled by
Leo; therefore, sunflower
motifs should please.

SUNFLOWER PEN

VIRGO

Instead of chocolates, give
your health-conscious
Virgoan lover a box
of crystallized fruit. Any
objects made from wood
will appeal to Virgos
because they are drawn
to natural materials.

AFRICAN
CARVED
WOOD
SPOON

CRYSTALLIZED
FRUIT

– TOKENS OF LOVE –

LIBRA

A board game will delight your Libran lover. Sentimental Librans also love music of all kinds and will be thrilled by a recording of a favorite piece.

VIOLIN

1930s
GAME
BOARD

SCORPIO

Scorpios will be delighted by an attractive leather belt or a sturdy, handsome wallet.

LEATHER
WALLET

19TH-CENTURY
ENGRAVING
OF AN EARLY
HOT-AIR
BALLOON

SAGITTARIUS

Adventurous Sagittarians love to travel. Your Sagittarian lover will be thrilled by the gift of an unusual experience, such as a flight in a hot-air balloon, and any travel-related object will be greatly appreciated.

ENAMELED
GLOBE
PILLBOX

CAPRICORN

Only the best will do for a fastidious Capricorn. Heavy antique glassware is guaranteed to appeal. If you would like to give your lover a plant, choose ivy.

IVY

HAND-THROWN
POTTERY MUG

VICTORIAN
GLASS
DECANTER

GIVING A BIRTHSTONE

SAPPHIRE

The most personal gift you can give your lover is the gem linked to his or her Sun sign.

ARIES: *diamond*
TAURUS: *emerald*
GEMINI: *agate* • CANCER: *pearl*
LEO: *ruby* • VIRGO: *sardonyx*
LIBRA: *sapphire* • SCORPIO: *opal*
SAGITTARIUS: *topaz*
CAPRICORN: *amethyst*
AQUARIUS: *aquamarine*
PISCES: *moonstone*

AQUARIUS

Unusual hand-thrown modern pottery and glassware will charm an unconventional Aquarian.

PISCES

Pisces is a water sign, and Pisceans love the sea. A decorative shell or piece of mother-of-pearl is guaranteed to delight your Piscean lover.

PEARLY
TURBAN
SHELL

YOUR PERMANENT RELATIONSHIP

PARTNERSHIP IS THE PERFECT STATE FOR A LIBRAN, AND YOU
MAY NOT FEEL COMPLETELY HAPPY AND FULFILLED UNTIL
YOU HAVE FORMED A PERMANENT RELATIONSHIP.

*L*ibrans are true romantics, forever in search of a secure and stable relationship with a partner to whom they can commit themselves entirely. However, this longing for romantic commitment does bring some dangers. There is a risk that you may rush too quickly and heedlessly into a permanent relationship – and you may act in haste only to repent at leisure.

This tendency to rush into a relationship occurs because Librans often do not feel entirely complete until they have found a partner. However, once settled within the framework of a happy relationship, Librans blossom – the sky turns blue, the sun comes out, and the birds sing.

You have a great need for balance and equality in your life and you will work hard to ensure that your relationship proceeds on an even keel.

You are likely to demand constant reassurance that your partner truly loves you. This may be exhausting for your lover, who may not realize the depth of your need for security. Try to understand that even in the happiest of partnerships, most people do not feel the need to make passionate declarations of love two or three times a day.

Although you are usually peace-loving, your longing for reassurance may lead you to cause arguments simply for the pleasure of kissing and making up afterward. Be warned – this is

A JOINT FUTURE
On a Sailing Ship, *by
Caspar David Friedrich,
shows a newly married
couple sailing into a
bright but unknown
future together.*

wearing for a partner,
and in the end it may
cause permanent
trouble.

Although you
feel more fulfilled
and content when
involved in a
relationship, try
to retain your
independence, and
do not submerge
your personality in
that of your lover.
If you ever feel discontented,
you may complain that you
have sacrificed far too much
for them. This is a completely
unjust claim, because you have
a tendency to devote yourself
entirely to your partner
whether they like it or not.

The worst Libran fault is a
tendency towards indecisiveness.
Resolve to take the initiative
more, and try to understand that
your partner may not always want
to be responsible for making
every decision that affects your
life together.

VENUS & MARS TABLES

THESE TABLES WILL ENABLE YOU TO DISCOVER WHICH SIGNS
VENUS AND MARS OCCUPIED AT THE MOMENT OF YOUR BIRTH.
TURN TO PAGES 24–45 TO INVESTIGATE THE QUALITIES OF THESE
SIGNS, AND TO FIND OUT HOW THEY WORK WITH YOUR SUN SIGN.

*T*he tables on pages 53–61
will enable you to discover
the positions of Venus and Mars at
the moment of your birth.

First find your year of birth
on the top line of the appropriate
table, then find your month of
birth in the left-hand column.
Where the column for your year
of birth intersects with the row
for your month of birth, you
will find a group of figures and
zodiacal glyphs. These figures
and glyphs show which sign of
the zodiac the planet occupied

on the first day of that month,
and any date during that month
on which the planet moved into
another sign.

For example, to ascertain the
position of Venus on May 10,
1968, run your finger down the
column marked 1968 until you
reach the row for May. The row
of numbers and glyphs shows
that Venus occupied Aries on
May 1, entered Taurus on May 4,
and then moved into Gemini on
May 28. Therefore, on May 10,
Venus was in Taurus.

*If you were born on a day when one of
the planets was moving into a new sign,
it may be impossible to determine your
Venus and Mars signs completely
accurately. If the characteristics described
on the relevant pages do not seem to
apply to you, read the interpretation of
the sign before and after. One of
these signs will be appropriate.*

ZODIACAL GLYPHS			
♈	Aries	♎	Libra
♉	Taurus	♏	Scorpio
♊	Gemini	♐	Sagittarius
♋	Cancer	♑	Capricorn
♌	Leo	♒	Aquarius
♍	Virgo	♓	Pisces

♀	1921	1922	1923	1924	1925	1926	1927	1928
JAN	1 ♒, 7 ♓	1 ♑, 25 ♒	1 ♏, ♐	1 ♒, 20 ♓	1 ♐, 15 ♑	1 ♒	1 ♑, 10 ♒	1 ♏, 5 ♐, 30 ♑
FEB	1 ♓, 3 ♈	1 ♒, 18 ♓	1 ♐, 7 ♑, 14 ♒	1 ♓, 14 ♈	1 ♑, 8 ♒	1 ♒	1 ♒, 3 ♓, 27 ♈	1 ♑, 23 ♒
MAR	1 ♈, 8 ♉	1 ♓, 14 ♈	1 ♑, 7 ♒	1 ♈, 10	1 ♒, 5 ♓, 29 ♈	1 ♒	1 ♈, ♉	1 ♒, 19 ♓
APR	1 ♉, 26 ♈	1 ♈, 7 ♉	1 ♓, 2 ♈, 27 ♉	1 ♉, 6 ♊	1 ♈, 22 ♉	1 ♒, 7 ♓	1 ♉, 17 ♊	1 ♓, 12 ♈
MAY	1 ♈	1 ♉, 2 ♊, 26 ♋	1 ♈, 22 ♉	1 ♊, ♋	1 ♉, 16 ♊	1 ♓, 7 ♈	1 ♊, 13 ♋	1 ♈, 7 ♉, 31 ♊
JUN	1 ♈, 3 ♉	1 ♊, 20 ♌	1 ♉, 16 ♊	1 ♋	1 ♊, 10 ♋	1 ♓, 3 ♈, 29 ♊	1 ♋, 9 ♌	1 ♊, 24 ♋
JUL	1 ♉, 9 ♊	1 ♌, 16 ♍	1 ♊, 11 ♋	1 ♋	1 ♋, 4 ♌, 29 ♍	1 ♊, 25 ♋	1 ♌, 8 ♍	1 ♋, 19 ♌
AUG	1 ♊, 6 ♋	1 ♍, 11 ♎	1 ♋, 4 ♌, 28 ♍	1 ♋	1 ♍, 23 ♎	1 ♋, 19 ♌	1 ♍	1 ♌, 12 ♍
SEP	1 ♌, 27 ♍	1 ♎, 8 ♏	1 ♍, 22 ♎	1 ♋, 8 ♌	1 ♎, 17 ♏	1 ♌, 12 ♍	1 ♍, 12 ♎	1 ♍, 5 ♎, 30 ♏
OCT	1 ♍, ♎	1 ♏, 11 ♐	1 ♎, 16 ♏	1 ♌, 12 ♍	1 ♏, 12 ♐	1 ♍, 6 ♎, 30 ♏	1 ♍	1 ♏, 24 ♐
NOV	1 ♎, 14 ♏	1 ♐, 29 ♏	1 ♏, 9 ♐	1 ♍, 3 ♎, 28 ♏	1 ♏, 7 ♐	1 ♏, 23 ♐	1 ♎, 10 ♏	1 ♐, 18 ♑
DEC	1 ♏, 8 ♐	1 ♏	1 ♐, 3 ♑, 27 ♒	1 ♏, 22 ♐	1 ♑, 6 ♒	1 ♐, ♑	1 ♎, 9 ♏	1 ♑, 13 ♒

♀	1929	1930	1931	1932	1933	1934	1935	1936
JAN	1 ♒, 7 ♓	1 ♑, 25 ♒	1 ♏, 4 ♐	1 ♒, 20 ♓	1 ♐, 15 ♑	1 ♒	1 ♑, 9 ♒	1 ♏, 4 ♐, 29 ♑
FEB	1 ♓, 3 ♈	1 ♒, 17 ♓	1 ♐, 7 ♑	1 ♓, 13 ♈	1 ♑, 8 ♒	1 ♒	1 ♒, 2 ♓, 27 ♈	1 ♑, 23 ♒
MAR	1 ♈, 9 ♉	1 ♓, 13 ♈	1 ♑, 6 ♒	1 ♈, 10	1 ♒, 4 ♓, 28 ♈	1 ♒	1 ♈, 23 ♉	1 ♒, 18 ♓
APR	1 ♉, 21 ♈	1 ♈, 7 ♉	1 ♓, 27 ♈	1 ♉, 6 ♊	1 ♈, 21 ♉	1 ♒, 7 ♓	1 ♉, 17 ♊	1 ♓, 12 ♈
MAY	1 ♈	1 ♊, 26 ♋	1 ♈, 22 ♉	1 ♊, ♋	1 ♉, 16 ♊	1 ♓, 7 ♈	1 ♊, 12 ♋	1 ♈, 6 ♉, 30 ♊
JUN	1 ♈, 4 ♉	1 ♋, 20 ♌	1 ♉, 15 ♊	1 ♋	1 ♊, 9 ♋	1 ♈, 3 ♉, 29 ♊	1 ♋, 8 ♌	1 ♊, 24 ♋
JUL	1 ♉, 9 ♊	1 ♌, 15 ♍	1 ♊, 10 ♋	1 ♋, 14 ♊, 29 ♋	1 ♋, 4 ♌, 28 ♍	1 ♊, 24 ♋	1 ♌, 8 ♍	1 ♋, 18 ♌
AUG	1 ♊, ♋	1 ♍, 11 ♎	1 ♋, 4 ♌, 28 ♍	1 ♋	1 ♍, 22 ♎	1 ♋, 18 ♌	1 ♍	1 ♌, 12 ♍
SEP	1 ♌, 26 ♍	1 ♎, 8 ♏	1 ♍, 21 ♎	1 ♋, 9 ♌	1 ♎, 16 ♏	1 ♌, 12 ♍	1 ♌, 12 ♎	1 ♍, 5 ♎, 29 ♏
OCT	1 ♍, 21 ♎	1 ♏, 13 ♐	1 ♎, 15 ♏	1 ♌, ♍	1 ♏, 12 ♐	1 ♍, 6 ♎, 30 ♏	1 ♍	1 ♏, 24 ♐
NOV	1 ♎, 14 ♏	1 ♐, 7 ♏	1 ♏, 8 ♐	1 ♍, 3 ♎, 28 ♏	1 ♏, 7 ♐	1 ♏, 23 ♐	1 ♎, 10 ♏	1 ♐, 17 ♑
DEC	1 ♏, 8 ♐, 31 ♑	1 ♏	1 ♐, 2 ♑, 26 ♒	1 ♏, 22 ♐	1 ♑, 6 ♒	1 ♐, 7 ♑	1 ♎, 17 ♏	1 ♑, 12 ♒

♀	1937	1938	1939	1940	1941	1942	1943	1944
JAN	1 ♒ 7 ♓	1 ♑ 24 ♒	1 ♏ 5 ♐	1 ♒ 19 ♓	1 ♐ 14 ♑	1 ♒	1 ♑ 9 ♒	1 ♏ 4 ♐ 29 ♑
FEB	1 ♓ 3 ♈	1 ♒ 17 ♓	1 ♐ 7 ♑	1 ♓ 13 ♈	1 ♑ 7 ♒	1 ♒	1 ♒ 2 ♓ 26 ♈	1 ♑ 22 ♒
MAR	1 ♈ 10 ♉	1 ♓ 13 ♈	1 ♑ 6 ♒	1 ♈ 9 ♉	1 ♒ 3 ♓ 28 ♈	1 ♒	1 ♈ 22 ♉	1 ♒ 18 ♓
APR	1 ♉ 15 ♈	1 ♈ 6 ♉ 30 ♊	1 ♓ 26 ♈	1 ♉ 5 ♊	1 ♈ 21 ♉	1 ♒ 7 ♓	1 ♉ 16 ♊	1 ♓ 11 ♈
MAY	1 ♈	1 ♊ 25 ♋	1 ♈ 21 ♉	1 ♊ 11 ♋	1 ♉ 15 ♊	1 ♓ 7 ♈	1 ♊ 12 ♋	1 ♈ 5 ♉ 30 ♊
JUN	1 ♈ 5 ♉	1 ♋ 19 ♌	1 ♉ 15 ♊	1 ♋	1 ♊ 8 ♋	1 ♈ 3 ♉ 28 ♊	1 ♋ 8 ♌	1 ♊ 23 ♋
JUL	1 ♉ 8 ♊	1 ♌ 15 ♍	1 ♊ 10 ♋	1 ♋ 6 ♊	1 ♋ 3 ♌ 28 ♍	1 ♊ 24 ♋	1 ♌ 8 ♍	1 ♋ 18 ♌
AUG	1 ♊ 5 ♋	1 ♍ 10 ♎	1 ♋ 3 ♌ 27 ♍	1 ♊ 2 ♋	1 ♍ 22 ♎	1 ♋ 18 ♌	1 ♍	1 ♌ 11 ♍
SEP	1 ♌ 26 ♍	1 ♎ 8 ♏	1 ♍ 21 ♎	1 ♋ 9 ♌	1 ♎ 16 ♏	1 ♌ 11 ♍	1 ♍	1 ♍ 4 ♎ 29 ♏
OCT	1 ♍ 19 ♎	1 ♏ 14 ♐	1 ♎ 15 ♏	1 ♌ 7 ♍	1 ♏ 13 ♐	1 ♍ 5 ♎ 29 ♏	1 ♍ 23 ♎	1 ♏ 23 ♐
NOV	1 ♎ 13 ♏	1 ♐	1 ♏ 8 ♐	1 ♍ 2 ♎ 27 ♏	1 ♐ 9 ♑	1 ♏ 22 ♐	1 ♎	1 ♐ 17 ♑
DEC	1 ♏ 7 ♐ 31 ♑	1 ♐ 20 ♏	1 ♐ 2 ♑ 26 ♒	1 ♏ 21 ♐	1 ♑ 6 ♒	1 ♐ 16 ♑	1 ♎ 9 ♏	1 ♑ 12 ♒

♀	1945	1946	1947	1948	1949	1950	1951	1952
JAN	1 ♒ 6 ♓	1 ♑ 23 ♒	1 ♏ 6 ♐	1 ♒ 19 ♓	1 ♐ 14 ♑	1 ♒	1 ♑ 8 ♒	1 ♏ 3 ♐ 28 ♑
FEB	1 ♓ 3 ♈	1 ♒ 16 ♓	1 ♐ 7 ♑	1 ♓ 12 ♈	1 ♑ 7 ♒	1 ♒	1 ♓ 25 ♈	1 ♑ 21 ♒
MAR	1 ♈ 12 ♉	1 ♓ 12 ♈	1 ♑ 6 ♒	1 ♈ 6 ♉	1 ♒ 3 ♓ 27 ♈	1 ♒	1 ♈ 22 ♉	1 ♒ 17 ♓
APR	1 ♉ 8 ♈	1 ♈ 6 ♉ 30 ♊	1 ♓ 26 ♈	1 ♉ 5 ♊	1 ♈ 20 ♉	1 ♒ 7 ♓	1 ♉ 16 ♊	1 ♓ 10 ♈
MAY	1 ♈	1 ♊ 25 ♋	1 ♈ 21 ♉	1 ♊ 11 ♋	1 ♉ 15 ♊	1 ♓ 7 ♈	1 ♊ 12 ♋	1 ♈ 5 ♉ 29 ♊
JUN	1 ♈ 5 ♉	1 ♋ 19 ♌	1 ♉ 14 ♊	1 ♋	1 ♊ 8 ♋	1 ♈ 3 ♉ 28 ♊	1 ♋ 8 ♌	1 ♊ 23 ♋
JUL	1 ♉ 8 ♊	1 ♌ 14 ♍	1 ♊ 9 ♋	1 ♋ 6 ♊	1 ♋ 2 ♌ 27 ♍	1 ♊ 23 ♋	1 ♌ 9 ♍	1 ♋ 17 ♌
AUG	1 ♊ 5 ♋ 31 ♌	1 ♍ 10 ♎	1 ♋ 3 ♌ 27 ♍	1 ♊ 2 ♋	1 ♍ 21 ♎	1 ♋ 17 ♌	1 ♍	1 ♌ 10 ♍
SEP	1 ♌ 25 ♍	1 ♎ 8 ♏	1 ♍ 20 ♎	1 ♋ 9 ♌	1 ♎ 15 ♏	1 ♌ 9 ♍	1 ♍	1 ♍ 4 ♎ 29 ♏
OCT	1 ♍ 17 ♎	1 ♏ 14 ♐	1 ♎ 14 ♏	1 ♌ 7 ♍	1 ♏ 11 ♐	1 ♍ 5 ♎ 29 ♏	1 ♍ 23 ♎	1 ♏ 23 ♐
NOV	1 ♎ 13 ♏	1 ♐	1 ♏ 8 ♐	1 ♍ 2 ♎ 27 ♏	1 ♐ 7 ♑	1 ♏ 22 ♐	1 ♎	1 ♐ 16 ♑
DEC	1 ♏ 7 ♐ 31 ♑	1 ♐ 25 ♏	1 ♐ 2 ♑ 26 ♒	1 ♏ 21 ♐	1 ♑ 6 ♒	1 ♐ 16 ♑	1 ♎ 9 ♏	1 ♑ 11 ♒

♀	1953	1954	1955	1956	1957	1958	1959	1960
JAN	1♒ 6♓	1♑ 7♒	1♏ 7♐	1♒ 18♓	1♐ 13♑	1♒	1♑ 8♒	1♏ 3♐ 28♑
FEB	1♓ 3♈	1♒ 16♓	1♐ 7♑	1♓ 12♈	1♑ 6♒	1♒	1♓ 25♈	1♑ 21♒
MAR	1♈ 15♉	1♓ 12♈	1♑ 5♒ 31♓	1♈ 8♉	1♒ 2♓ 26♈	1♒	1♈ 21♉	1♒ 16♓
APR	1♈	1♈ 5♉ 29♊	1♓ 25♈	1♉ 5♊	1♈ 19♉	1♒ 7♓	1♉ 15♊	1♓ 10♈
MAY	1♈	1♊ 24♋	1♈ 20♉	1♊ 9♋	1♉ 14♊	1♓ 6♈	1♊ 11♋	1♈ 4♉ 29♊
JUN	1♈ 6♉	1♋ 18♌	1♉ 14♊	1♋	1♊ 7♋	1♈ 2♉ 27♊	1♋ 22♌	1♊ 22♋
JUL	1♉ 8♊	1♌ 14♍	1♊ 9♋	1♊	1♋ 2♌ 27♍	1♊ 22♋	1♌ 9♍	1♋ 16♌
AUG	1♊ 5♋ 31♌	1♍ 9♎	1♋ 2♌ 26♍	1♊ 6♋	1♍ 21♎	1♋ 16♌	1♍	1♌ 9♍
SEP	1♌ 25♍	1♎ 7♏	1♍ 19♎	1♋ 9♌	1♎ 15♏	1♌ 10♍	1♍ 21♎ 26♏	1♍ 3♎ 28♏
OCT	1♍ 19♎	1♏ 24♐ 28♏	1♎ 13♏	1♌ 7♍	1♏ 11♐	1♍ 3♎ 28♏	1♍	1♏ 22♐
NOV	1♎ 12♏	1♏	1♏ 6♐	1♎ 26♏	1♏ 6♐	1♏ 21♐	1♍ 10♎	1♐ 16♑
DEC	1♏ 6♐ 30♑	1♏	1♑ 25♒	1♏ 20♐	1♐ 7♑	1♐ 15♑	1♎ 8♏	1♑ 11♒

♀	1961	1962	1963	1964	1965	1966	1967	1968
JAN	1♒ 6♓	1♑ 22♒	1♏ 7♐	1♒ 17♓	1♐ 13♑	1♒	1♑ 7♒ 31♓	1♏ 2♐ 27♑
FEB	1♓ 3♈	1♒ 15♓	1♐ 6♑	1♓ 11♈	1♑ 6♒	1♒ 7♑ 26♒	1♓ 24♈	1♑ 21♒
MAR	1♈	1♓ 11♈	1♑ 5♒ 31♓	1♈ 8♉	1♒ 2♓ 26♈	1♒	1♈ 21♉	1♒ 16♓
APR	1♈	1♈ 4♉ 29♊	1♓ 25♈	1♉ 5♊	1♈ 19♉	1♒ 7♓	1♉ 15♊	1♓ 9♈
MAY	1♈	1♊ 24♋	1♈ 19♉	1♊ 10♋	1♉ 13♊	1♓ 6♈	1♊ 11♋	1♈ 4♉ 28♊
JUN	1♈ 6♉	1♋ 18♌	1♉ 13♊	1♋ 18♊	1♊ 7♋	1♈ 27♉	1♋ 7♌	1♊ 21♋
JUL	1♉ 8♊	1♌ 13♍	1♊ 8♋	1♊	1♋ 26♌	1♊ 22♋	1♌ 9♍	1♋ 16♌
AUG	1♊ 4♋ 30♌	1♍ 9♎	1♋ 26♌	1♊ 6♋	1♌ 20♍	1♋ 16♌	1♍	1♌ 9♍
SEP	1♌ 24♍	1♎ 8♏	1♍ 18♎	1♋ 9♌	1♍ 14♎	1♌ 9♍	1♍ 10♎	1♍ 3♎ 27♏
OCT	1♍ 18♎	1♏	1♎ 13♏	1♌ 6♍	1♎ 10♏	1♍ 3♎ 27♏	1♎ 2♏	1♏ 22♐
NOV	1♎ 12♏	1♏	1♏ 6♐ 30♑	1♍ 25♎	1♏ 6♐	1♏ 20♐	1♎ 10♏	1♏ 15♐
DEC	1♏ 6♐ 29♑	1♏	1♑ 24♒	1♏ 20♐	1♑ 8♒	1♐ 14♑	1♎ 8♏	1♑ 10♒

– VENUS TABLES –

♀	1969	1970	1971	1972	1973	1974	1975	1976
JAN	1♒ 5♓	1♑ 22♒	1♏ 8♐	1♒ 16♓	1♐ 12♑	1♒ 30♑	1♑ 17♒ 31♓	1♏ 2♐ 27♑
FEB	1♓ 3♈	1♒ 15♓	1♐ 6♑	1♓ 11♈	1♑ 5♒	1♑	1♓ 24♈	1♑ 20♒
MAR	1♈	1♓ 11♈	1♑ 5♒ 30♓	1♈	1♓ 25♈	1♒	1♈ 20♉	1♒ 15♓
APR	1♈	1♈ 4♉ 28♊	1♓ 24♈	1♉ 4♊	1♈ 19♉	1♒ 7♓	1♉ 14♊	1♓ 9♈
MAY	1♈	1♊ 23♋	1♈ 19♉	1♊ 11♋	1♉ 13♊	1♓ 5♈	1♊ 10♋	1♈ 3♉ 27♊
JUN	1♈ 6♉	1♋ 17♌	1♉ 13♊	1♋ 12♊	1♊ 6♋	1♈ 26♉	1♋ 7♌	1♊ 21♋
JUL	1♉ 7♊	1♌ 13♍	1♊ 7♋ 31♌	1♊	1♌ 24♍	1♉ 20♊	1♍ 22♎	1♋ 15♌
AUG	1♊ 4♋ 30♌	1♍ 25♎	1♌ 25♍	1♊ 7♋	1♍ 18♎	1♊ 15♋	1♍	1♌ 8♍
SEP	1♌ 24♍	1♎ 18♏	1♍ 18♎	1♋ 8♌	1♎ 11♏	1♋ 9♌	1♌ 3♍	1♍ 2♎ 26♏
OCT	1♍ 18♎	1♏	1♎ 12♏	1♌ 6♍ 31♎	1♏ 5♐ 30♑	1♌ 3♍ 27♎	1♍	1♏ 21♐
NOV	1♎ 11♏	1♏	1♏ 5♐ 30♑	1♎ 25♏	1♑ 24♒	1♎ 20♏	1♍ 10♎	1♐ 14♑
DEC	1♏ 5♐ 29♑	1♏	1♑ 24♒	1♏ 19♐	1♒	1♏ 14♐	1♎ 7♏	1♑ 10♒

♀	1977	1978	1979	1980	1981	1982	1983	1984
JAN	1♒ 5♓	1♑ 21♒	1♏ 8♐	1♒ 16♓	1♐ 12♑	1♒ 24♑	1♑ 6♒ 30♓	1♏ 2♐ 26♑
FEB	1♓ 3♈	1♒ 14♓	1♐ 6♑	1♓ 10♈	1♑ 5♒ 28♓	1♑	1♓ 23♈	1♑ 20♒
MAR	1♈	1♓ 10♈	1♑ 4♒ 29♓	1♈	1♓ 23♈	1♒	1♈ 20♉	1♒ 15♓
APR	1♈	1♈ 3♉ 28♊	1♓ 23♈	1♉ 4♊	1♈ 18♉	1♒ 7♓	1♉ 14♊	1♓ 8♈
MAY	1♈	1♊ 22♋	1♈ 18♉	1♊ 13♋	1♉ 12♊	1♓ 5♈ 31♉	1♊ 10♋	1♈ 3♉ 27♊
JUN	1♈ 7♉	1♋ 17♌	1♉ 12♊	1♋ 6♊	1♊ 6♋ 30♌	1♉ 26♊	1♋ 7♌	1♊ 21♋
JUL	1♉ 7♊	1♌ 12♍	1♊ 7♋ 31♌	1♊	1♌ 25♍	1♊ 21♋	1♌ 21♍	1♋ 15♌
AUG	1♊ 5♋ 29♌	1♍ 25♎	1♌ 25♍	1♊ 7♋	1♍ 19♎	1♋ 15♌	1♍ 28♌	1♌ 8♍
SEP	1♌ 23♍	1♎ 18♏	1♍ 18♎	1♋ 8♌	1♎ 13♏	1♌ 8♍	1♌	1♍ 2♎ 26♏
OCT	1♍ 17♎	1♏	1♎ 12♏	1♌ 5♍ 31♎	1♏ 9♐	1♌ 2♍ 26♎	1♌ 6♍	1♏ 21♐
NOV	1♎ 11♏	1♏	1♏ 5♐ 29♑	1♎ 25♏	1♏ 6♑	1♎ 19♏	1♍ 10♎	1♐ 14♑
DEC	1♏ 4♐ 28♑	1♏	1♑ 23♒	1♏ 19♐	1♑ 9♒	1♏ 12♐	1♎ 7♏	1♑ 10♒

– VENUS TABLES –

♀	1985	1986	1987	1988	1989	1990	1991	1992
JAN	1 ♒ · 5 ♓	1 ♑ · 21 ♒	1 ♏ · 8 ♐	1 ♒ · 16 ♓	1 ♐ · 11 ♑	1 ♒ · 17 ♑	1 ♑ · 6 ♒ · 30 ♓	1 ♐ · 26 ♑
FEB	1 ♓ · 3 ♈	1 ♒ · 14 ♓	1 ♐ · 6 ♑	1 ♓ · 10 ♈	1 ♑ · 4 ♒ · 28 ♓	1 ♑	1 ♓ · 23 ♈	1 ♑ · 19 ♒
MAR	1 ♈	1 ♓ · 9 ♈	1 ♑ · 7 ♒ · 28 ♓	1 ♈ · 7 ♉	1 ♓ · 24 ♈	1 ♑ · 4 ♒	1 ♈ · 19 ♉	1 ♒ · 14 ♓
APR	1 ♈	1 ♈ · 3 ♉ · 27 ♊	1 ♓ · 23 ♈	1 ♉ · 4 ♊	1 ♈ · 17 ♉	1 ♒ · 7 ♓	1 ♉ · 13 ♊	1 ♓ · 7 ♈
MAY	1 ♈	1 ♊ · 22 ♋	1 ♈ · 18 ♉	1 ♊ · 18 ♋ · 27 ♊	1 ♉ · 12 ♊	1 ♓ · 4 ♈ · 31 ♉	1 ♊ · 9 ♋	1 ♈ · 2 ♉ · 26 ♊
JUN	1 ♈ · 7 ♉	1 ♋ · 16 ♌	1 ♉ · 12 ♊	1 ♊	1 ♊ · 5 ♋ · 30 ♌	1 ♉ · 25 ♊	1 ♋ · 7 ♌	1 ♊ · 20 ♋
JUL	1 ♉ · 7 ♊	1 ♌ · 12 ♍	1 ♊ · 6 ♋ · 31 ♌	1 ♊	1 ♌ · 24 ♍	1 ♊ · 20 ♋	1 ♌ · 11 ♍	1 ♋ · 14 ♌
AUG	1 ♊ · 3 ♋ · 28 ♌	1 ♍ · 8 ♎	1 ♌ · 24 ♍	1 ♊ · 7 ♋	1 ♍ · 18 ♎	1 ♋ · 13 ♌	1 ♍ · 22 ♌	1 ♌ · 7 ♍
SEP	1 ♌ · 23 ♍	1 ♎ · 8 ♏	1 ♍ · 17 ♎	1 ♋ · 8 ♌	1 ♎ · 13 ♏	1 ♌ · 9 ♍	1 ♌	1 ♎ · 25 ♏
OCT	1 ♍ · 17 ♎	1 ♏	1 ♎ · 11 ♏	1 ♌ · 9 ♍ · 30 ♎	1 ♏ · 9 ♐	1 ♍ · 2 ♎ · 26 ♏	1 ♌ · 7 ♍	1 ♏ · 20 ♐
NOV	1 ♎ · 10 ♏	1 ♏	1 ♏ · 4 ♐ · 28 ♑	1 ♎ · 24 ♏	1 ♐ · 6 ♑	1 ♏ · 19 ♐	1 ♍ · 9 ♎	1 ♐ · 14 ♑
DEC	1 ♏ · 4 ♐ · 28 ♑	1 ♏	1 ♑ · 23 ♒	1 ♏ · 18 ♐	1 ♑ · 10 ♒	1 ♐ · 13 ♑	1 ♎ · 7 ♏	1 ♑ · 9 ♒

♀	1993	1994	1995	1996	1997	1998	1999	2000
JAN	1 ♒ · 4 ♓	1 ♑ · 20 ♒	1 ♏ · 8 ♐	1 ♒ · 15 ♓	1 ♐ · 10 ♑	1 ♒ · 10 ♑	1 ♑ · 5 ♒ · 29 ♓	1 ♐ · 25 ♑
FEB	1 ♓ · 3 ♈	1 ♒ · 13 ♓	1 ♐ · 5 ♑	1 ♓ · 9 ♈	1 ♑ · 4 ♒ · 28 ♓	1 ♑	1 ♓ · 22 ♈	1 ♑ · 19 ♒
MAR	1 ♈	1 ♓ · 9 ♈	1 ♑ · 3 ♒ · 29 ♓	1 ♈ · 6 ♉	1 ♓ · 24 ♈	1 ♑ · 5 ♒	1 ♈ · 19 ♉	1 ♒ · 14 ♓
APR	1 ♈	1 ♈ · 2 ♉ · 27 ♊	1 ♓ · 23 ♈	1 ♉ · 4 ♊	1 ♈ · 17 ♉	1 ♒ · 7 ♓	1 ♉ · 13 ♊	1 ♓ · 7 ♈
MAY	1 ♈	1 ♊ · 21 ♋	1 ♈ · 17 ♉	1 ♊	1 ♉ · 11 ♊	1 ♓ · 4 ♈ · 30 ♉	1 ♊ · 9 ♋	1 ♈ · 2 ♉ · 26 ♊
JUN	1 ♈ · 7 ♉	1 ♋ · 15 ♌	1 ♉ · 11 ♊	1 ♊	1 ♊ · 4 ♋ · 29 ♌	1 ♉ · 25 ♊	1 ♋ · 6 ♌	1 ♊ · 19 ♋
JUL	1 ♉ · 6 ♊	1 ♌ · 12 ♍	1 ♊ · 6 ♋ · 30 ♌	1 ♊	1 ♌ · 24 ♍	1 ♊ · 20 ♋	1 ♌ · 13 ♍	1 ♋ · 14 ♌
AUG	1 ♊ · 2 ♋ · 28 ♌	1 ♍ · 8 ♎	1 ♌ · 23 ♍	1 ♊ · 8 ♋	1 ♍ · 18 ♎	1 ♋ · 14 ♌	1 ♍ · 16 ♌	1 ♌ · 7 ♍
SEP	1 ♌ · 22 ♍	1 ♎ · 8 ♏	1 ♍ · 17 ♎	1 ♋ · 8 ♌	1 ♎ · 12 ♏	1 ♌ · 7 ♍	1 ♌	1 ♎ · 25 ♏
OCT	1 ♍ · 16 ♎	1 ♏	1 ♎ · 11 ♏	1 ♌ · 8 ♍ · 29 ♎	1 ♏ · 9 ♐	1 ♍ · 2 ♎ · 25 ♏	1 ♌ · 8 ♍	1 ♏ · 20 ♐
NOV	1 ♎ · 9 ♏	1 ♏	1 ♏ · 4 ♐ · 28 ♑	1 ♎ · 23 ♏	1 ♐ · 6 ♑	1 ♏ · 18 ♐	1 ♍ · 10 ♎	1 ♐ · 13 ♑
DEC	1 ♏ · 3 ♐ · 27 ♑	1 ♏	1 ♑ · 22 ♒	1 ♏ · 17 ♐	1 ♑ · 12 ♒	1 ♐ · 12 ♑	1 ♎ · 6 ♏	1 ♑ · 9 ♒

♂	1921	1922	1923	1924	1925	1926	1927	1928	1929	1930
JAN	1 ♒ 5 ♓	1 ♏	1 ♓ 21 ♈	1 ♏ 19 ♐	1 ♈	1 ♐	1 ♉	1 ♐ 19 ♑	1 ♊	1 ♑
FEB	1 ♓ 13 ♈	1 ♏ 18 ♐	1 ♈	1 ♐	1 ♈ 5 ♉	1 ♐ 9 ♑	1 ♉ 22 ♊	1 ♑ 28 ♒	1 ♊	1 ♑ 6 ♒
MAR	1 ♈ 25 ♉	1 ♐	1 ♈ 8 ♉	1 ♐ 6 ♑	1 ♉ 24 ♊	1 ♑ 23 ♒	1 ♊	1 ♒	1 ♊ 10 ♋	1 ♒ 17 ♓
APR	1 ♉	1 ♐	1 ♉ 16 ♊	1 ♑ 24 ♒	1 ♊	1 ♒	1 ♊ 17 ♋	1 ♒ 7 ♓	1 ♋	1 ♓ 24 ♈
MAY	1 ♉ 6 ♊	1 ♐	1 ♊ 30 ♋	1 ♒	1 ♊ 9 ♋	1 ♒ 3 ♓	1 ♋	1 ♓ 16 ♈	1 ♋ 13 ♌	1 ♈
JUN	1 ♊ 18 ♋	1 ♐	1 ♋	1 ♒	1 ♋ 26 ♌	1 ♓ 15 ♈	1 ♋ 6 ♌	1 ♈ 26 ♉	1 ♌	1 ♈ 3 ♉
JUL	1 ♋	1 ♐	1 ♋ 16 ♌	1 ♒	1 ♌	1 ♈	1 ♌ 25 ♍	1 ♉	1 ♌ 4 ♍	1 ♉ 14 ♊
AUG	1 ♋ 3 ♌	1 ♐	1 ♌	1 ♒	1 ♌ 12 ♍	1 ♈ 12 ♉	1 ♍	1 ♉ 9 ♊	1 ♍ 21 ♎	1 ♊ 28 ♋
SEP	1 ♌ 19 ♍	1 ♐ 13 ♑	1 ♍	1 ♒	1 ♍ 28 ♎	1 ♉	1 ♍ 10 ♎	1 ♊	1 ♎	1 ♋
OCT	1 ♍	1 ♑ 30 ♒	1 ♍ 18 ♎	1 ♒	1 ♎	1 ♉	1 ♎ 26 ♏	1 ♊ 3 ♋	1 ♎ 6 ♏	1 ♋ 20 ♌
NOV	1 ♍ 6 ♎	1 ♒	1 ♎	1 ♒ 13 ♓	1 ♎ 13 ♏	1 ♉	1 ♏	1 ♋	1 ♏ 18 ♐	1 ♌
DEC	1 ♎ 26 ♏	1 ♒ 11 ♓	1 ♎ 4 ♏	1 ♓ 19 ♈	1 ♏ 28 ♐	1 ♉	1 ♏ 8 ♐	1 ♋ 20 ♊	1 ♐ 29 ♑	1 ♌

♂	1931	1932	1933	1934	1935	1936	1937	1938	1939	1940
JAN	1 ♌	1 ♑ 18 ♒	1 ♍	1 ♒	1 ♎	1 ♒ 14 ♓	1 ♎ 5 ♏	1 ♓ 30 ♈	1 ♏ 29 ♐	1 ♓ 4 ♈
FEB	1 ♌ 16 ♋	1 ♒ 25 ♓	1 ♍	1 ♒ 4 ♓	1 ♎	1 ♓ 22 ♈	1 ♏	1 ♈	1 ♐	1 ♈ 17 ♉
MAR	1 ♋ 30 ♌	1 ♓	1 ♍	1 ♓ 14 ♈	1 ♎	1 ♈	1 ♏ 13 ♐	1 ♈ 12 ♉	1 ♐ 21 ♑	1 ♉
APR	1 ♌	1 ♓ 3 ♈	1 ♍	1 ♈ 22 ♉	1 ♎	1 ♈	1 ♐	1 ♉ 23 ♊	1 ♑	1 ♉ 19 ♊
MAY	1 ♌	1 ♈ 12 ♉	1 ♍	1 ♉	1 ♎	1 ♈ 12 ♉	1 ♐ 14 ♏	1 ♊	1 ♑ 24 ♒	1 ♊ 17 ♋
JUN	1 ♌ 10 ♍	1 ♉ 22 ♊	1 ♍	1 ♉ 2 ♊	1 ♎	1 ♉ 25 ♊	1 ♏	1 ♊ 7 ♋	1 ♒	1 ♋
JUL	1 ♍	1 ♊	1 ♍ 6 ♎	1 ♊ 15 ♋	1 ♎ 29 ♏	1 ♊	1 ♏	1 ♋ 22 ♌	1 ♒ 21 ♑	1 ♋ 3 ♌
AUG	1 ♎	1 ♊ 4 ♋	1 ♎ 26 ♏	1 ♋ 30 ♌	1 ♏	1 ♊ 10 ♋	1 ♏ 8 ♐	1 ♌	1 ♑	1 ♌ 19 ♍
SEP	1 ♎ 17 ♏	1 ♋ 20 ♌	1 ♏	1 ♌	1 ♏ 16 ♐	1 ♋ 26 ♌	1 ♐ 30 ♑	1 ♌ 7 ♍	1 ♑ 24 ♒	1 ♍
OCT	1 ♏ 30 ♐	1 ♌	1 ♏ 9 ♐	1 ♌ 18 ♍	1 ♐ 28 ♑	1 ♌ 20 ♍	1 ♑ 25 ♒	1 ♍	1 ♒	1 ♍ 5 ♎
NOV	1 ♐	1 ♌ 13 ♍	1 ♐ 19 ♑	1 ♍	1 ♑	1 ♍ 25 ♎	1 ♒	1 ♍ 11 ♎	1 ♒ 19 ♓	1 ♎ 20 ♏
DEC	1 ♐ 10 ♑	1 ♍	1 ♑ 28 ♒	1 ♍ 11 ♎	1 ♑ 7 ♒	1 ♎	1 ♒ 21 ♓	1 ♎ 11 ♏	1 ♓	1 ♏

♂	1941	1942	1943	1944	1945	1946	1947	1948	1949	1950
JAN	1 ♏ 4 ♐	1 ♈ 11 ♉	1 ♐ 26 ♑	1 ♊	1 ♐ 5 ♑	1 ♋	1 ♑ 25 ♒	1 ♍	1 ♑ 4 ♒	1 ♎
FEB	1 ♐ 17 ♑	1 ♉	1 ♑	1 ♊	1 ♑ 14 ♒	1 ♋	1 ♒	1 ♍ 12 ♌	1 ♒ 11 ♓	1 ♎
MAR	1 ♑	1 ♉ 7 ♊	1 ♑ 8 ♒	1 ♊ 29 ♋	1 ♒ 25 ♓	1 ♋	1 ♒ 4 ♓	1 ♌	1 ♓ 21 ♈	1 ♎ 28 ♍
APR	1 ♑ 2 ♒	1 ♊ 26 ♋	1 ♒ 17 ♓	1 ♋	1 ♓	1 ♋ 22 ♌	1 ♓ 11 ♈	1 ♌	1 ♈ 30 ♉	1 ♍
MAY	1 ♒ 16 ♓	1 ♋	1 ♓ 27 ♈	1 ♋ 22 ♌	1 ♓ 3 ♈	1 ♌	1 ♈ 21 ♉	1 ♌ 18 ♍	1 ♉	1 ♍
JUN	1 ♓	1 ♋ 14 ♌	1 ♈	1 ♌	1 ♈ 11 ♉	1 ♌ 20 ♍	1 ♉	1 ♍	1 ♉ 10 ♊	1 ♍ 11 ♎
JUL	1 ♓ 2 ♈	1 ♌	1 ♈ 7 ♉	1 ♌ 12 ♍	1 ♉ 23 ♊	1 ♍	1 ♊	1 ♍ 17 ♎	1 ♊ 23 ♋	1 ♎
AUG	1 ♈	1 ♍	1 ♉ 23 ♊	1 ♍ 29 ♎	1 ♊	1 ♍ 9 ♎	1 ♊ 13 ♋	1 ♎	1 ♋	1 ♎ 10 ♏
SEP	1 ♈	1 ♍ 17 ♎	1 ♊	1 ♎	1 ♊ 7 ♋	1 ♎ 24 ♏	1 ♋	1 ♎ 3 ♏	1 ♋ 7 ♌	1 ♏ 25 ♐
OCT	1 ♈	1 ♎	1 ♊	1 ♎ 2 ♏	1 ♋	1 ♏	1 ♌	1 ♏ 17 ♐	1 ♌ 27 ♍	1 ♐
NOV	1 ♈	1 ♎ 2 ♏	1 ♊	1 ♏ 25 ♐	1 ♏ 11 ♐	1 ♏ 6 ♐	1 ♌	1 ♐ 26 ♑	1 ♍	1 ♐ 6 ♏
DEC	1 ♈	1 ♏ 15 ♐	1 ♊	1 ♐	1 ♌ 26 ♋	1 ♐ 17 ♑	1 ♍	1 ♑	1 ♍ 26 ♎	1 ♑ 15 ♒

♂	1951	1952	1953	1954	1955	1956	1957	1958	1959	1960
JAN	1 ♒ 22 ♓	1 ♎ 20 ♏	1 ♓	1 ♏	1 ♓ 15 ♈	1 ♏ 14 ♐	1 ♈ 28 ♉	1 ♐	1 ♉	1 ♐ 14 ♑
FEB	1 ♓	1 ♏	1 ♓ 8 ♈	1 ♏ 9 ♐	1 ♈ 26 ♉	1 ♐ 28 ♑	1 ♉	1 ♐ 3 ♑	1 ♉ 10 ♊	1 ♑ 23 ♒
MAR	1 ♓ 2 ♈	1 ♏	1 ♈ 20 ♉	1 ♐	1 ♉	1 ♑	1 ♉ 17 ♊	1 ♑ 17 ♒	1 ♊	1 ♒
APR	1 ♈ 10 ♉	1 ♏	1 ♉	1 ♐ 12 ♑	1 ♉ 10 ♊	1 ♑ 14 ♒	1 ♊	1 ♒ 27 ♓	1 ♊ 10 ♋	1 ♒ 2 ♓
MAY	1 ♉ 21 ♊	1 ♏	1 ♊	1 ♑	1 ♊ 26 ♋	1 ♒	1 ♊ 4 ♋	1 ♓	1 ♋	1 ♓ 11 ♈
JUN	1 ♊	1 ♏	1 ♊ 14 ♋	1 ♑	1 ♋	1 ♒ 3 ♓	1 ♋ 21 ♌	1 ♓ 7 ♈	1 ♋ 2 ♌	1 ♈ 20 ♉
JUL	1 ♊ 3 ♋	1 ♏	1 ♋ 29 ♌	1 ♑ 3 ♐	1 ♋ 11 ♌	1 ♓	1 ♌	1 ♈ 21 ♉	1 ♌ 20 ♍	1 ♉
AUG	1 ♋ 18 ♌	1 ♏ 27 ♐	1 ♌	1 ♐ 24 ♑	1 ♌ 27 ♍	1 ♓	1 ♌ 8 ♍	1 ♉	1 ♍	1 ♉ 2 ♊
SEP	1 ♌	1 ♐	1 ♌ 14 ♍	1 ♑	1 ♍	1 ♓	1 ♍ 24 ♎	1 ♉ 21 ♊	1 ♍ 5 ♎	1 ♊ 21 ♋
OCT	1 ♌ 5 ♍	1 ♐ 12 ♑	1 ♍	1 ♑ 21 ♒	1 ♍ 13 ♎	1 ♓	1 ♎	1 ♊ 29 ♋	1 ♎ 21 ♏	1 ♋
NOV	1 ♍ 24 ♎	1 ♑ 21 ♒	1 ♎	1 ♒	1 ♎ 29 ♏	1 ♓	1 ♎ 8 ♏	1 ♋	1 ♏	1 ♋
DEC	1 ♎	1 ♒ 30 ♓	1 ♎ 20 ♏	1 ♒ 4 ♓	1 ♏	1 ♓ 6 ♈	1 ♏ 23 ♐	1 ♉	1 ♏ 3 ♐	1 ♋

– MARS TABLES –

♂	1961	1962	1963	1964	1965	1966	1967	1968	1969	1970
JAN	1 ♋	1 ♑	1 ♌	1 13 ♑ ♒	1 ♍	1 30 ♒ ♓	1 ♎	1 9 ♒ ♓	1 ♏	1 24 ♓ ♈
FEB	1 5 7 ♋ ♊ ♋	1 2 ♑ ♒	1 ♌	1 20 ♒ ♓	1 ♍	1 ♓	1 12 ♎ ♏	1 17 ♓ ♈	1 25 ♏ ♐	1 ♈
MAR	1 ♋	1 12 ♒ ♓	1 ♌	1 29 ♓ ♈	1 ♍	1 9 ♓ ♈	1 31 ♏ ♎	1 28 ♈ ♉	1 ♐	1 7 ♈ ♉
APR	1 ♋	1 19 ♓ ♈	1 ♌	1 ♈	1 ♍	1 17 ♈ ♉	1 ♎	1 ♉	1 ♐	1 18 ♉ ♊
MAY	1 6 ♋ ♌	1 28 ♈ ♉	1 ♌	1 7 ♈ ♉	1 ♍	1 28 ♉ ♊	1 ♎	1 8 ♉ ♊	1 ♐	1 ♊
JUN	1 28 ♌ ♍	1 ♉	1 3 ♌ ♍	1 17 ♉ ♊	1 29 ♍ ♎	1 ♊	1 ♎	1 21 ♊ ♋	1 ♐	1 2 ♊ ♋
JUL	1 ♍	1 9 ♉ ♊	1 27 ♍ ♎	1 30 ♊ ♋	1 ♎	1 11 ♊ ♋	1 19 ♎ ♏	1 ♋	1 ♐	1 18 ♋ ♌
AUG	1 17 ♍ ♎	1 22 ♊ ♋	1 ♎	1 ♋	1 20 ♎ ♏	1 25 ♋ ♌	1 ♏	1 5 ♋ ♌	1 ♐	1 ♌
SEP	1 ♎	1 ♋	1 12 ♎ ♏	1 15 ♋ ♌	1 ♏	1 ♌	1 10 ♏ ♐	1 21 ♌ ♍	1 21 ♐ ♑	1 3 ♌ ♍
OCT	1 2 ♎ ♏	1 11 ♋ ♌	1 25 ♏ ♐	1 ♌	1 4 ♏ ♐	1 12 ♌ ♍	1 23 ♐ ♑	1 ♍	1 ♑	1 20 ♍ ♎
NOV	1 13 ♏ ♐	1 ♌	1 ♐	1 6 ♌ ♍	1 14 ♐ ♑	1 ♍	1 ♑	1 9 ♍ ♎	1 4 ♑ ♒	1 ♎
DEC	1 24 ♐ ♑	1 ♌	1 5 ♐ ♑	1 ♍	1 23 ♑ ♒	1 4 ♍ ♎	1 2 ♑ ♒	1 30 ♎ ♏	1 15 ♒ ♓	1 6 ♎ ♏

♂	1971	1972	1973	1974	1975	1976	1977	1978	1979	1980
JAN	1 23 ♏ ♐	1 ♈	1 ♐	1 ♉	1 21 ♐ ♑	1 ♊	1 ♑	1 26 ♌ ♋	1 21 ♑ ♒	1 ♍
FEB	1 ♐	1 10 ♈ ♉	1 12 ♐ ♑	1 27 ♉ ♊	1 ♑	1 ♊	1 9 ♑ ♒	1 ♋	1 28 ♒ ♓	1 ♍
MAR	1 12 ♐ ♑	1 27 ♉ ♊	1 27 ♑ ♒	1 ♊	1 3 ♑ ♒	1 18 ♊ ♋	1 20 ♒ ♓	1 ♋	1 ♓	1 12 ♍ ♌
APR	1 ♑	1 ♊	1 ♒	1 20 ♊ ♋	1 11 ♒ ♓	1 ♋	1 28 ♓ ♈	1 10 ♋ ♌	1 7 ♓ ♈	1 ♌
MAY	1 3 ♑ ♒	1 12 ♊ ♋	1 8 ♒ ♓	1 ♋	1 21 ♓ ♈	1 16 ♋ ♌	1 ♈	1 ♌	1 16 ♈ ♉	1 4 ♌ ♍
JUN	1 ♒	1 28 ♋ ♌	1 21 ♓ ♈	1 9 ♋ ♌	1 ♈	1 ♌	1 6 ♈ ♉	1 14 ♌ ♍	1 26 ♉ ♊	1 ♍
JUL	1 ♒	1 ♌	1 ♈	1 27 ♌ ♍	1 ♉	1 7 ♌ ♍	1 18 ♉ ♊	1 ♍	1 ♊	1 11 ♍ ♎
AUG	1 ♒	1 15 ♌ ♍	1 12 ♈ ♉	1 ♍	1 14 ♉ ♊	1 24 ♍ ♎	1 ♊	1 4 ♍ ♎	1 8 ♊ ♋	1 29 ♎ ♏
SEP	1 ♒	1 ♍	1 ♉	1 12 ♍ ♎	1 ♊	1 ♎	1 ♋	1 20 ♎ ♏	1 25 ♋ ♌	1 ♏
OCT	1 ♒	1 ♎	1 30 ♉ ♈	1 28 ♎ ♏	1 17 ♊ ♋	1 8 ♎ ♏	1 27 ♋ ♌	1 ♏	1 ♌	1 12 ♏ ♐
NOV	1 6 ♒ ♓	1 15 ♎ ♏	1 ♈	1 ♏	1 26 ♋ ♊	1 21 ♏ ♐	1 ♌	1 2 ♏ ♐	1 20 ♌ ♍	1 22 ♐ ♑
DEC	1 26 ♓ ♈	1 30 ♏ ♐	1 24 ♈ ♉	1 11 ♏ ♐	1 ♊	1 ♐	1 ♌	1 12 ♐ ♑	1 ♍	1 31 ♑ ♒

♂	1981	1982	1983	1984	1985	1986	1987	1988	1989	1990
JAN	1 ♒	1 ♎	1 ♒ 17 ♓	1 ♎ 11 ♏	1 ♓	1 ♏	1 ♓ 8 ♈	1 ♏ 9 ♐	1 ♈ 19 ♉	1 ♐ 30 ♑
FEB	1 ♒ 7 ♓	1 ♎	1 ♓ 25 ♈	1 ♏	1 ♓ 3 ♈	1 ♏ 2 ♐	1 ♈ 21 ♉	1 ♐ 22 ♑	1 ♉	1 ♑
MAR	1 ♓ 17 ♈	1 ♎	1 ♈	1 ♏	1 ♈ 15 ♉	1 ♐ 28 ♑	1 ♉	1 ♑	1 ♉ 11 ♊	1 ♑ 12 ♒
APR	1 ♈ 25 ♉	1 ♎	1 ♈ 5 ♉	1 ♏	1 ♉ 26 ♊	1 ♑	1 ♉ 6 ♊	1 ♑ 7 ♒	1 ♊ 29 ♋	1 ♒ 21 ♓
MAY	1 ♉	1 ♎	1 ♉ 17 ♊	1 ♏	1 ♊	1 ♑	1 ♊ 21 ♋	1 ♒ 22 ♓	1 ♋	1 ♓ 31 ♈
JUN	1 ♉ 5 ♊	1 ♎	1 ♊ 29 ♋	1 ♏	1 ♊ 9 ♋	1 ♑	1 ♋	1 ♓	1 ♋ 17 ♌	1 ♈
JUL	1 ♊ 18 ♋	1 ♎	1 ♋	1 ♏	1 ♋ 25 ♌	1 ♑	1 ♋ 7 ♌	1 ♓ 13 ♈	1 ♌	1 ♈ 13 ♉
AUG	1 ♋	1 ♎ 3 ♏	1 ♋ 14 ♌	1 ♏ 18 ♐	1 ♌	1 ♑	1 ♌ 23 ♍	1 ♈	1 ♌ 3 ♍	1 ♉ 31 ♊
SEP	1 ♋ 2 ♌	1 ♏ 20 ♐	1 ♌ 30 ♍	1 ♐	1 ♌ 10 ♍	1 ♑	1 ♍	1 ♈	1 ♍ 20 ♎	1 ♊
OCT	1 ♌ 21 ♍	1 ♐	1 ♍	1 ♐ 5 ♑	1 ♍ 28 ♎	1 ♑ 9 ♒	1 ♍ 9 ♎	1 ♈ 24 ♓	1 ♎	1 ♊
NOV	1 ♍	1 ♑	1 ♍ 18 ♎	1 ♑ 16 ♒	1 ♎	1 ♒ 26 ♓	1 ♎ 24 ♏	1 ♓ 2 ♈	1 ♎	1 ♊
DEC	1 ♍ 16 ♎	1 ♑ 10 ♒	1 ♎	1 ♒ 25 ♓	1 ♎ 15 ♏	1 ♓	1 ♏	1 ♈	1 ♏ 18 ♐	1 ♊ 14 ♉

♂	1991	1992	1993	1994	1995	1996	1997	1998	1999	2000
JAN	1 ♉ 21 ♊	1 ♐ 9 ♑	1 ♋	1 ♑ 28 ♒	1 ♍ 23 ♌	1 ♑ 9 ♒	1 ♍ 3 ♎	1 ♒ 25 ♓	1 ♎ 26 ♏	1 ♒ 4 ♓
FEB	1 ♊	1 ♑ 18 ♒	1 ♋	1 ♒	1 ♌	1 ♒ 15 ♓	1 ♎	1 ♓	1 ♏	1 ♓ 12 ♈
MAR	1 ♊	1 ♒ 28 ♓	1 ♋	1 ♒ 7 ♓	1 ♌	1 ♓ 25 ♈	1 ♎ 9 ♍	1 ♓ 5 ♈	1 ♏	1 ♈ 23 ♉
APR	1 ♊ 3 ♋	1 ♓	1 ♋ 27 ♌	1 ♓ 15 ♈	1 ♌	1 ♈	1 ♍	1 ♈ 13 ♉	1 ♏	1 ♉
MAY	1 ♋ 27 ♌	1 ♓ 6 ♈	1 ♌	1 ♈ 24 ♉	1 ♌ 26 ♍	1 ♈ 3 ♉	1 ♍	1 ♉ 24 ♊	1 ♏ 6 ♎	1 ♉ 4 ♊
JUN	1 ♌	1 ♈ 15 ♉	1 ♌ 23 ♍	1 ♉	1 ♍	1 ♉ 12 ♊	1 ♍	1 ♊	1 ♎	1 ♊ 16 ♋
JUL	1 ♌ 16 ♍	1 ♉ 27 ♊	1 ♍	1 ♉ 4 ♊	1 ♍ 21 ♎	1 ♊ 26 ♋	1 ♎	1 ♊ 6 ♋	1 ♎ 5 ♏	1 ♋
AUG	1 ♍	1 ♊	1 ♍ 12 ♎	1 ♊ 17 ♋	1 ♎	1 ♋	1 ♎ 14 ♏	1 ♋ 21 ♌	1 ♏	1 ♌
SEP	1 ♎	1 ♊ 12 ♋	1 ♎ 27 ♏	1 ♋	1 ♎ 7 ♏	1 ♋ 10 ♌	1 ♏ 29 ♐	1 ♌	1 ♏ 3 ♐	1 ♌ 17 ♍
OCT	1 ♎ 17 ♏	1 ♋	1 ♏	1 ♋ 5 ♌	1 ♏ 21 ♐	1 ♍	1 ♐	1 ♌ 7 ♍	1 ♐ 17 ♑	1 ♍
NOV	1 ♏ 29 ♐	1 ♋	1 ♏ 9 ♐	1 ♌	1 ♐ 30 ♑	1 ♍	1 ♐ 9 ♑	1 ♍ 27 ♎	1 ♑ 26 ♒	1 ♍ 4 ♎
DEC	1 ♐	1 ♋	1 ♐ 20 ♑	1 ♌ 12 ♍	1 ♑	1 ♍	1 ♑ 18 ♒	1 ♎	1 ♒	1 ♎ 23 ♏